The Girl Inside Me

For all who suffered sexual abuse
or trauma as children

Queen Chisa

Love Ganelin

Thanks for the support

Dear Chrissy

Love Grandma

Thank you for the support

The Girl Inside Me

For all who suffered sexual abuse
or trauma as children

poems by
Javelin Hardy

DANCING MOON PRESS
NEWPORT, OREGON

The Girl Inside Me—
For all who suffered sexual abuse or trauma as children

ISBN: 978-1-945587-05-4 – (paperback)
Library of Congress Control Number: 2017932519
Book editing, design & production: *Carla Perry*
Cover design & production: *Sarah Gayle Art*

Hardy, Javelin
1. Poetry; 2. Poems-healing and recovery; 3. Poems-childhood sexual
abuse and trauma; 4. Poems for the Black Queen; 5. Poems-
relationships; 6. Poems-survival
I. TITLE

First Edition

Contents

Section 6 The Invisible Black Woman

Section 7 Pain Owns Your Heart

Section 8 What Is Happening To The Black Family?

Section 9 Healing From The Heart

Endorsement

The Girl Inside Me is a heartfelt book and very moving. As a writer, I understand how complex it can be putting oneself out there to the public, but people are looking for real people, with real situations that can heal others and restore hope. Javelin Hardy's collection of poems does exactly that. Even the book's title immediately speaks to the reader, opening curiosity about the direction the book will take.

As I read Hardy's poems, numerous emotions surfaced and her words allowed me to transform into her and feel her experiences. The titles of her poems anchored me in place and time. For instance, "He Touched Me," immediately brought to mind a scared little girl with pigtails, ankle socks, and a teddy bear held by one ear. A tall man standing with pointy shoes and smelling of cigar smoke. I felt her anger, hurt, resentment, pain, and redemption. Her poems allowed me to walk in the shoes of that small, frightened girl as she experienced things no little girl should ever go through.

The little girl inside of Javelin Hardy has matured into a beautiful, powerful woman capable of healing others using her personal experience and training in her therapeutic profession. And what more of a blessing it will be as this collection of poems, *The Girl Inside Me,* goes further out into the world and touches the lives of so many more.

—Kimberly Robinson Green, Author of
Her Cry—Her Prayer—Her Praise
and *Encouraged To Finish*

Dedication

I dedicate this book to my mother, Jeroldine "Puddin" Hardy, who was, and still is, the Black Opal Queen of my Universe.

The brown in the soil, earth, rocks, and trees
The blue in the ski, ocean, sea, and rivers
The green in the leaves, fruit, and grass
You are my spirit, my heartbeat, my laugh, my knowledge.
You were and still are my
Black Opal Queen.
August 29, 2012 RIP.

To all the children who are now adults who suffered childhood sexual abuse or trauma.
"We are survivors."

By His stripes we are healed.

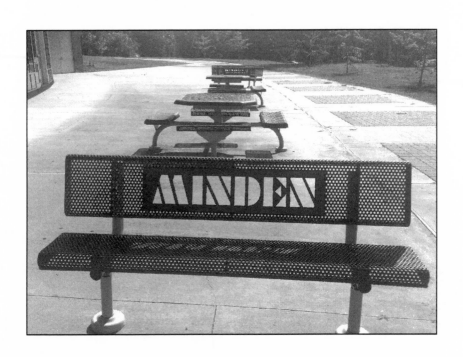

Section 1
Minden

Minden

Being raised in a small Southern town has its positive and negative sides. On the positive side, most Southern people I know are the best cooks and lovers I've meet. Maybe it's all the Soul Food, but we put our soul into everything we do—from the Zydeco dancing to the gumbo, the rhythm illuminates our spirit. Oh, how I want to suck my fingers when I smash my hot water cornbread in my collard and mustard greens. Puddin never used a fork when she ate her greens. Please add a little vinegar and a sliced green onion for taste.

Folks think we are stupid because of the country accent, but I grew up with some of the smartest people and had the most educated African American teachers.

The negative side is that everyone knows everyone's business and it's hard to get in trouble as a child because word spread so quick, your mother knew what you did at school or church before she got home from work. You also knew who was creeping with who; and who was at the drive in liquor store and shouting in church the next day... was it from the wine or from the conviction? I always wonder.

As a little girl, my mother ventured off to California, and the 1970s was a time when a country girl could get in a lot of trouble. Let's just say my mother was a fox and she kept what she caught. I watched my mother and that is where I learned how to date, how to carry myself as a lady, and realize the power women had with the "poonanie."

I've been writing since I've been eight years old. I've kept most of my poetry. I use to journal all my pain and confused feelings. Writing saved my life because the pain wanted me to die.

13

Now, it's time to share some personal things that led to where I am today as a woman. I'm still continuing to find out who I am as a Black Queen, continuing to demand to be truly loved the way black people used to love. So sit back and ride along on my journey with the little girl inside me who is now a woman.

Home

Hardy's Kindergarten, Jacks Store – Craton Hill
Mrs. Harris Library
New Light Baptist Church
Rev Coleman
He rose on the 3rd day
With all Power in his Hands
He never said a mumbling word
Marching in on the Midnight Train to Glory
Sunny-boy—Ricky Alstock
Walking around Heaven All Day
Gloria's magic fingers on the piano
Ushers at their post—signals
Communion Sunday
Mr. Snook Cosby could fix anything
Made of iron—washing machine to a car
Lay a new roof on your home
Ms. Josie had the best farm-fresh eggs in town
Mrs. Tot made the best 7-Up cake and chilidogs
Penny candy
Papa working in the garden—Smokey could count to 10
Smokey led the parade every year
Stewart Elementary—Lowe Middle School
Webster Junior High
Minden High School
Best teachers in the world
Track and field
Football team
The Corner
Dairy Queen
Cotton's Chicken
The Rec

Mrs. Jackson drove the bus and open up the pool
During the summer
Shinny
Turk's washhouse and dry cleaners
Cadillac Street
Rebecca Street
J.L. Jones
West Street
Homer Road
Walmart
Dixie Inn
Piggly Wiggly
Mr. Twister
Shell Plan
Town-N-Country
What you going to do with your life child?
College or the military?
You can't live here without a job.

Cranton Hill vs. Wood Street

I didn't know social and economic difference existed in my small
country town until I got in high school
I'd already experienced growing up in grade school having a best
friend who was white, and then she stopped talking to me

When we went to middle school, I hung with all the black kids and
she with the white kids
I had family who lived on the other side of town where black
people lived and they lived in brick houses
I grew up in a wooden framed house with faded white paint and a
roof that leaked

I found out what the word "boosie" meant
Black folks that act like they got something
Too good for their own folks
Black folks that wouldn't let their kids date poor kids
When they thought they were too good
Blacks folks that tried to speak proper
And wiped their ass the same way
I wiped mine
With toilet paper.

Eugene Anderson, my grandfather

Eugene Anderson

Who knew his D.O.B?
He told me he was given a birth date
But wasn't sure when he was born
Papa told me he picked cotton as a small child
And worked in the salt mines
Papa couldn't read or write so he signed his name with an
X

You couldn't beat him out of his money
He was his own man
He made horseshoes, knives, and other metal tools
I guess you can call him a
Blacksmith

I grew up with his horse, Smokey
Smokey wore a straw hat and could count by patting the ground
With his foot
He also knew how to say no and yes
Papa rode Smokey in the parade every year in
Minden

Papa grew his own food in the garden and had chickens
Papa owned his own land
Papa taught me how to save
Papa taught me how to make healing teas and salves
Papa was a rare man who lived to the young age of
93
You were the only grandfather I knew

I look for men who resemble your character and attributes
I have yet to meet any.

Vera Hardy, my grandmother

Hardy's Kindergarten

Vera Hardy
Had the first African American preschool and kindergarten
In the town of Minden, Louisiana
What a pleasure to see photos
Of children who graduated from my grandmother's school

I was told Vera would bite your finger and twist your ear
If you cut up in school
I was also told you were taught not only education, but how to
Carry yourself as a Black Child
With respect, dignity, and value

I didn't get the chance to meet my grandmother

My mother told me I took after my grandmother
Because I always had children in my home
Teaching and feeding children in my neighborhood

Vera Hardy's education is a legacy I wish to continue
As a Social Worker and Adjunct Professor.

Crack Cocaine

Crack Cocaine pretty much destroyed 80s kid's homes
We lost our mothers and fathers
Some recovered but some never returned

Crack came into my mother's life and I didn't recognize her
She lost herself and the man she was with
Took her down a longer road that she wanted to travel on

Crack Cocaine
Put evil spirits in the smartest, sweetest people
I knew people who sold everything in their home for a
Rock
Sold kitchen cabinets, stole from their mother
Stole your TV out your home
And then tried to sell it to you

Samuel Jackson danced for his mama in a movie
To get some money for a Rock

Crack Cocaine destroyed the Black Family
I had to fight the spirit of crack cocaine...
I fought my mother because of
Crack Cocaine
I stopped speaking to my mother for almost five years because of
Crack Cocaine

Section 2
Introducing The Child

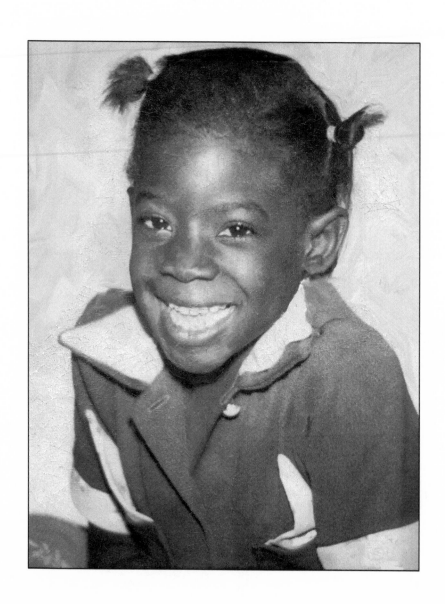

He Touched Me

I don't understand why you touched me the way you did. I was only six years old. I know we were trying to do what we heard the adults do. I could hear my mother moaning, sounds that were so loud and so confusing. I saw the look in the men's eyes when they wanted my mother. I started getting the same look when I was a woman.

You were twelve and I was six
You had your way with me
I lie helpless. Afraid
It was confusing to me
You were twelve and I was six
This was the life of Cali.

The Babysitter

Who knew girls were predators?
When I was seven, my babysitter wanted to play 'Find the Navel'
Turns out the navel
was in the same place the twelve year old boy had
Found

Is it a secret that most black children
Have been sexually abused or molested
And we see it as part of growing up
And exploring sexuality?

Who told you it was okay to touch something or someone
That didn't belong to you?
It's amazing the behaviors repeated from unhealthy love examples

You were taught to take a child's innocence
You didn't realize what you did
But you opened up a soul of lust
That confused the purity of love.

Why You So Mean?

Damn she is mean and evil when she wakes up!
Well, you would be mean and evil too if you had dreams
Every night of hands touching you in places
That should never have been touched as a
Child

You would be mean and evil too if you still saw
The person who touched you and
They acted like they didn't do anything because
They were a teenager now and had boyfriends

Yes, I still remember what you did to me
And I will never forget it
You taught me the wrong kind of
Love.

I Felt That In My Stomach

At age twelve, I had long legs, black skin and I thought I was ugly
But all of a sudden, my body started changing
I had small breast and a high bottie
Boys noticed my bottie
And sometimes grown men said stuff
Until I told them who my father
Was

My first kiss with a boy
Blew me away and since I had been touched as a child
I thought it was okay when I got a boyfriend
So I went all the way
That was at age twelve.

I Said, "No!"

It was 1986—you were my first boyfriend
After we moved to Portland
It was in high school and you invited me to your birthday party
A basement party!
Being a country girl, I've never been to a basement
Party

Both alcohol and drugs were available
But I didn't partake in
Either

After everyone left, I stayed to help you
Clean
When you asked did I have a birthday
Gift
I smiled and gave you the card and cologne
Because we'd just meet and had been dating only a couple of
Weeks

When it got late, I asked if you could walk me home
And you said, "Yes, after I get my present."
You wouldn't allow me to leave
And decided to take what you thought was your present
I said, "No!"
Then I lay helpless and lifeless
I said, "No!"

Boyfriends

I grew up with LL Cool J, New Edition, Curtis Blow
And Missy Elliott
LL sang, "I need Love," well, so did I

New Edition sang, "I need a girlfriend & Candy Girl"
'I thought they were singing to me!

Missy sung, "Let me show you how to work it!"
Once I got the taste of the dick
I had to have it all the time
I didn't realize I was trying to fill a void
The dick couldn't fill
It was only a
Dick

At that time, I didn't understand
Love
I just knew
Lust
And a
Dick.

The Little Girl Inside Me

There is a little girl inside of me
Trapped, afraid and wanting to be set free.
But I'm 33 now—
What is this little girl doing inside of me?

Life is moving on but the pain inside hasn't been set free
What is he doing molesting me?

I just want to play, to play Pattie-Cake, Ring-Around-The-Rosy
And Hop-Scotch Double Dutch
If you have a
Rope.

Why is that man watching me?
Why are these kids touching me?
"Just leave me alone!"

Didn't you care who babysit us, or did you trust everyone?
All she wants to do is party
All the time
Party all the time

Why is he humping on me?
The little Girl Inside of Me
Has she been set free?

Section 3
The Secret

The Secret

At age 33, I decided to tell my mother about all the childhood
Sexual abuse I had experienced
My mother wasn't ready
Her response was, *You make me feel as if*
I'm on the Ricky Lake or Oprah Show
I didn't expect my mother
To get it, or be ready to take responsibility
For not protecting me and raising me in a healthy
Environment

I don't hate you, Mother
I forgave you a long time ago
I just needed to let you know
So I could be on my journey
To heal

Months later, you stood in the doorway of
My home and said, *I'm so proud of you*
And I wish I wouldn't had ran different men in and out of my house
I wish I could have fulfilled all my dreams

You're a good mother and I'm
Proud of you
I'm so sorry.

No More Sheets

Juanita Bynum's book, *No More Sheets,*
Shifted a spirit inside of me
That placed me on a spiritual journey

I realized I have connected my soul with a lot of lost lustful spirits
And could have become addicted to like-minded people and spirits

I've come to realize that a person could feel me
And I could feel them, no matter
Where they were!

That was a scary, dangerous place for me
I was not only battling my
Flesh
But dangerous spiritual warfare as well.

Seven Years

I didn't date for seven years because I was so tired of
Bad relationships
And being hurt
I couldn't take it anymore

And my prayer was for God to show me
Someone who wanted to love
And not just want me for my body

During those seven years, I discovered I was beautiful
I discovered I didn't know
Myself
I discovered I didn't know what love looked
Like

I discovered I had issues with men
Especially my father
I had issues with my mother
But I discovered how to love
When I had children.

Abandonment

My first experience of being abounded was when I got pregnant
with my first son and his father didn't want anything to do with
him. My son is now 26 and he still hasn't met his father.

The man lived on Wood Street
I never understood how he could create a life
And not want to be a part of the life of the child born

Not all advice from your mother is good, you know
My child showed me love
Love that the six-year-old girl was searching for,
Who is now
18

Love is patient, love is kind. It does not envy, it does not boast
It is not proud, it does not dishonor others
It is not self-seeking. It is not easily angered
It keeps no record of wrongs

Love does not delight in evil, but
Rejoices with the truth
It always protects, always trust, always hopes
Always perseveres
Love never fails

I Corinthians 13:1
"Jonathan"
You are a gift from God.

He's Your Child Too

We were high school sweethearts
You'd already moved on to college, but you took me to my
Senior prom
In between, a child was born
You couldn't accept that I was pregnant
You wanted me to
Have an abortion

Your father accepted I was with child
Your mother wanted to know if
The child was yours because you
Already had one daughter

Soon after, I realized it wasn't love
I left it alone
Now my son is five. He will be 6 in
December
He prays for his father
And every day he ask me,
*"Mom when am I going to meet my
Dad?"*

When he grows up to be a strong black man
I pray he will not hate his dad for not accepting him
You know, John
He's your child too.

Wanting Love And Not Knowing What Love Looked Like

Wesley.
There's no attachment in relationships
When people are unhealthy and
Hurt

It's a sexual relationship
A physical attachment
Then a child is
Born

Then you realize you don't know me
And I don't know you

After my second child
I rededicated my life to Christ
Because I felt so lost and damaged
I couldn't afford to be hurt anymore
So I poured my time into my sons
Who carried the traits of anger
And abandonment from their
Fathers.

I Had Five Children, But Kept Only Two

I couldn't afford mentally to have five children
Without fathers who didn't want children
You wanted my body but not our
Children
I had five children, but kept only two.

Section 4
The Transition

The Little Girl Is Now A Woman

For the first time in my life, I felt beautiful
The little, ugly, black girl with pony tails
Is now a woman

What was it that made me feel ugly?
The mean words we called each other back then?
Maybe it was how I saw myself, and low self-esteem
Or how the media portrayed black women

The little girl doesn't skip, hop, or double-dutch anymore
She walks gracefully and sore
The little girl's black skin is now a deep dark, smooth, silk chocolate
That makes men slack at the knees
The little girl used to giggle all the time
But now the woman laughs in a sexy, alluring way to her man
She enjoys his company and conversation

The little girl's ponytails are dark-black locks now
That bounce when she walks
Her teeth are pearl white and light up the world with sunshine
Her long, skinny legs are big, round and sexy
Connected to her Coke bottle
Figure

The flat chest is now round breasts enough to feed her young
She knows who she is, no sex symbol, not to be used and taken
Advantage of. But to raise her young, love her husband
And obey God

The little girl is now a Black Queen.

I Am Eve

I am a child of God
I am an Egyptian Queen
I am an African Queen

I am a woman who bares children
I am a mother
I am a daughter
I am a sister

I am a child inside a woman's body
I am a working woman
I am a student
I am a father to my sons
I am a promise keeper
I am a promise seeker

I am a tired old woman
Who has been in the cotton field
From sun up to sun down
With bleeding fingers and blistered feet
Who do you think I am?

And if I was a slave
What would you sell me for?
How much am I worth?

I Have Finally Found The Man I Love

I have finally found the man I love
Let me introduce you

His name is Jesus
The Lilly of the Valley
The bright morning star
He not only gives me flowers in season
But also live music
Not an organ, piano, or flute
But a bird
Water flowing from waterfalls, oceans, rain
From the sky
And when He smiles, the entire world
Is brighter
Whenever I look, I see something
That reminds me how close He is to
Me
I'm so happy I've found that
Special Man

You see, I've been looking
And he's been there all the
Time.

He Said He Wasn't Emotionally Available

I met a man who I learned to love.
When I first met him, he said he was not emotionally
Available
Wow, I thought, *the first honest brother*
I've ever met
I let him know it had been seven years
And if he wanted me, he had to
Be mentally and spiritually
Available

As time went on, I said,
"The boy inside of you has abandonment issues
Trust Issues
Mama Issues
Addiction Issues you battled
But you still have Crackish
Tendencies
You are afraid
You say you would never get married."
I said, "There is nothing I can do for
You"

But you triggered something in me and took me back to that
Unsafe place where I had been refusing to return
See, I had a little girl to protect
And you, little boy, tried to
Pull her in.

Why The One Who Loves You The Most Ends up Hurting You

Mother, daughter—a man enters her life
Makes her feel good, makes her feel the way a women
Should feel
Held. Touched. Kissed. Loved.
So special, it can't be described

Drink, smoke—move on to bigger and better things

A woman sometimes does things to make her man happy
Or she's around people who do things she's not accustomed to
She doesn't want to be left out

Is this what it's like, being an adult, a mother, a lover?
Responsibilities don't mean as much as they used to
She has a young child to look after, 'cause the older daughter
Left!

What should I do?
My mother left me—I feel empty, left out!
What about Mother's Day?
I still love my mother,
I've done all I could
I have my own life to live

The years come, the years go
But Crack will always have a
Show.

To Be Real

To Stay Real is to be Real
Because to Be Real you got to
Be Real
If you're not going to be Real
Don't expect me to believe
You
Trust
You
Or have faith in You
I need Real Love
Real Time
Real Peace
Real Joy
And a 4-Real God
To help me to stay Real
Lord Jesus, help me
To be Real.

Misunderstanding A Black Woman

You say, I look mean and angry—
Shit
I have so much on my mind... I have to be still to hear
God
I have to tune out—drama...TV...social media...the corrupt
World
Pay bills... raise children... support my lost brothers...
Recover every time a black family... is killed
Or separated...
So please, don't judge my face
You couldn't handle half the shit going through my mind
Worried...
Will my sons be shot by the police?
Or black-on-black crime?
Will they get caught up in the criminal justice system?
Worried...
They will get caught up in drugs or alcohol
That they won't continue the family legacy...
The traditions, morals, values...
And raise their children with the Word of
God
God just freed me from the job of Worry
The misunderstandings of the Black Woman

Don't read my face
Try understanding my
Heart.

Section 5
My Soul Looks Back And Wonders

Just When I Thought I Was Breathing On My Own

For Hayward Demison

You are the air I breathe
Just when I thought I was running all alone
You are the air I breathe
Just when I thought I was gasping my last breath
You are the air I breathe
You brought me back
You gave me a second chance
You are my light, my force, my shield
You are the air I breathe

You sent an angel just when I needed help
You spoke life into my body
Breath
Life
Hope
Love
You are the air I breathe.

You Left Me Today
August 29, 2012

Today, I sit motionlessly looking at your lifeless body
You left me today
Today, I see no more spirit, no more smile
You left me today
Who will carry your throne?
Who will reign in your place, Black Queen?
You left me today
I will carry on in your place.

You left me today.

I Have Two Holes In My Heart
October 16, 2012

My mom and my man.
My mom left without a choice
My man left without a voice
that spoke unity and one accord to my spirit.
You have no idea what is the meaning of real love
You say you love me but afraid to unite as one
You have no idea why Christ died for his son
He emptied Himself and gave His life so we may live
How do you leave something you love?
Because you're afraid to give yourself as one
I lost my mom and my man....
One had no choice.

Jeroldine

Pudding pie kissed the boys and made them cry
Raised three kids without batting any eye
Cooked sweet potato pie that made you cry
Had more strength than a Proverbs 31 woman
Could whoop you and pick you up with one hand
Had to be a strong man to take Jeroldine's Hand
Proverb 31:15
She got up while it was still dark
She provided food for her family and portions to friends
She set about her work vigorously
Her arms were strong for her tasks
Proverbs 31: 20
She opened her arms to the poor
And extended her hands to the needy
She was clothed with strength and dignity
She laughed at the days to come
She spoke with wisdom and faithful instructions
She watched over the affairs of her household
And did not eat the bread of idleness
Her children arise and call her blessed
Her husband also, and he praises her
Courage, wisdom, love and strength...
Jeroldine, you're a strong Black Queen

Love you, mom
Javelin.

I've Lost Myself

I lost myself along the way, Father and I'm sorry
I caught a glimpse of your love, and somehow I lost it
I allowed a man to catch my eye because
I wanted so bad to be loved and validated by man
Well, seven years have passed and I'm still not loved by man

I've lost myself in school, work, and kids
So I wouldn't have the time
To look up and see I still don't have man
Well, my sons are now 21 and 18
And you're preparing me for a journey alone

You can lead
I pray I'll be Abram
And obey without questions
As to where I'm going

You see, I lost myself
Help me, Lord, find my way back to you.

Sail Away, My Friend

Dedicated to John Harlin.
You are—were—will be forever—my friend!

Sail Away My Friend
Sail away to a sea that never ends
Sail away to blue skis and winds
That sing songs of love and happiness

Sail Away My Friend
To a place where there is no pain or suffering
To a place where all are loved and cared for
To seas that roar and will never spit you out
To seas you will sail and never come a shore

Sail Away My Friend
To where love starts and has no end
Sail Away My Friend.

Heaven Must Be Like This!

For Diane Wade

Your smile and spirit illuminated this place
Heaven must be like this...

The sound of your laughter and the embrace of your hugs
Heaven must be like this!
Your eyes spoke hidden thoughts... dreams and ideas
Heaven must be like this...

You accepted everyone, and worked with those
The world turns away
Heaven must be like this...
You had a heart so big
You were able to love everyone...
I want to learn this!

You will be missed but your spirit lives on
Your legacy lives on!
Heaven must be like this....

*I know everyone celebrates things differently and we have
our own healing process for grief.
Well, I write poetry on the side
and wanted to share this with you all!*

Your Spirit Is Like A Breath Of Fresh Air

One day I was walking to my school in the neighborhood
The Holy Spirit and I had a personal conversation
And I felt God's presence

Your Spirit blows right through me
I can't get enough of your spirit
It burns within me
You are like fire, shut up in my bones
Your Spirit illuminates my spirit
Your light shines right through me
I can't get enough of you

You are a halo over my spirit
Your love overpowers me
I can't get enough of you

I desperately seek you
I can't imagine living without you
You pull me back in when we disconnected
Your spirit and I are one.

My Soul Looks Back And Wonders How I Made It Over

In the words of Curtis Blow
"It's like a jungle sometimes;
It makes me wonder how I keep from
Going under"

I'm trying not to lose my head because I feel like on edge
I say, God keeps me from going under
My Soul looks back and wonder how I survived
Childhood issues, being a young mother, raising two black
Men

My soul looks back and wonders how I made it over
God's grace and love: renewal, refreshing, healing
Forgiveness—Christ dying for me

My soul looks back and shouts
Through the jungle
Runs through the jungle
Prays through the jungle
Conquers the jungle

My soul looks back and wonders how I made it over.

Things Hidden In Our Heart
August 27, 2015

When you think you've gotten over something or someone, a trigger can reawaken all the pain and disappointments you've experienced. There are hidden compartments in my heart. God, please remove disappointments, painful relationships, men I've committed myself to without You, and selfish relationships that didn't have anything to do with you.

The Wild Journey

On a quest, a voyage, I set out on my own. Without a map, I was
lost in the sea of love. I thought I was ready to travel. I've been
studying. I've had my quiet time. I fasted and I prayed. And still I
went shipwreck. I cast my anchor and I was attacked. I was
ambushed by lust when desire became buried oh-so-quickly. My
children were wild pirates attacking the curious sailors. They didn't
even give them a chance. They were willing to take what the men
had, but weren't willing to share our ship. So now we set sail again
with the wind in our hair, not knowing where were going but we
have peace for this new voyage.

Unleash Me Please/Remove Your Hold/ Remove Your Spell

I want to be released by you. Please just let me go and when you leave, please don't come back. Don't see me as a failure, see me as growth. Growth to trust growth. Growth to heal. I just want to be free from the chains that are binding me. You are holding me hostage with your unresolved issues and pain. I'm sorry. I'm sorry your mother gave you away, and I'm sorry for the pain she caused. Please don't take it out on me what she did to you, and what she couldn't give to you. I tried too.
Please release me.

The Keys To My ♥
August 17, 2015

Lord, I give you the keys to my heart.
My heart has many doors.
Doors of pain
Abuse
Sickness
Grief
Fatherlessness
And abandonment.
Lord, I give you the keys to my heart.

Section 6
The Invisible Black Woman

The Invisible Black Woman

The Invisible black woman
Was once seen as an Egyptian Queen Mother
The Nile River was the length of your love and grace
The black essence of your skin
Reflected the long hours you toiled in the sun
Your body bore your children and held your husband's
Hands
The Earth was hers
And she grew food for her young
And food for her village

Africa is now the home of women who can twerk the best
Women who have the biggest breasts

Queen, get back to your roots!
Stopping scarring your body by Botox and tattoos
Why must we enlarge what we naturally have?
Why is the Queen Invisible?

If I Were An Ancestor

If I could be an ancestor from history, I would be Harriet Tubman
She freed the slaves
More could had been free if they would had believed they were free
If I could be an ancestor, I would be
Maya Angelou. She was raped as a little girl
Became mute, then spoke in front of
Thousands using colorful words forming tapestries and paintings
She wrote poems of love, affirmations
Still I rise
Jill Scott
I'm more than what is between my thighs
I am the woman at the well who had many husbands
And Jesus spoke into my life
And told me all about my sins. Then
He said I wouldn't thirst again
He said, he got that drink so that I wouldn't thirst again
I was told God lives in me. He sets us free
I am that Iyanla Vanzant
I can hear, see, and feel your pain
I can show you how to speak to that thing
Do you know why you are a Black Queen?
Queen—are you that video Queen?
Project Queen
Welfare Queen
Master of all trades, jack of none Queen
Master's degree Queen
Holding it down working—school
Are you a lost, Queen?
What say you, Queen?
Claim your throne!
If I were an Ancestor.

From The Slave Block To The Settlement Check

I read that by law, once a family receives a civil settlement
From the police
They can no longer speak on the case
Well, the grave is speaking
The loved one you took a check for
Wants to know why you are not
Speaking on their behalf, to have the person
Charged with manslaughter
Murder
You see, we were already lined up and
Measured
From our ass, thighs, breast size
How well the African male would
Breed
We were separated, and our children went with another family
While the father was sold to the highest bidder
It was bad enough our tongues were cut
Because we refused to speak the language
They raped our women
Took away our God, and made us
Worship the one you painted white
Its 2016, and you're still a paycheck slave
Taking checks from the master
Who killed you husband, father, brother, and uncle
I read that by law once a family receives a civil settlement
From the police
You can no longer speak on the case
Well the grave is crying
Out!

Can I Get A Man?

Can I get a man into my life who wants to stay?
Who wants to love?
Who won't run?
A man who loves God, for real?
Who will look out for me?
Who is not selfish but self-less?
Who will bless
Cover
Protect
Cherish me
Can I get a man to protect and listen to me?
Care and provide for me?
Is that too much to ask?

If Looks Could Kill... She Texted Me!

If she could only see what's going on inside my heart, I thought…
Heart of despair, relationship disappointments, and family betrayal
She may not understand or see things as I see them because of the
age and culture differences
You see…you and I grew up at different times in different regions
I'm a Southern Belle, and you're a Northwesterner…
What's the difference? you ask
If a Southern woman raises another man's kids—
even if they don't marry—we are family
If I've fed, clothed, and made loved to a man you are now married
to—we are all family

Now!
It may sound crazy to you—I was there when the kids felt
lost, abandoned, and ignored
Because their father complained of being tied down and bothered
by his kids
The line you crossed was breaking the unspoken rule of
"Spiritual sisters," dating the same man
is no different than my little sister dating an "ex" of mine
So when you see me, don't expect a warm greeting or
congratulations
I'm still in shock that the entire marriage went down.
I'm just confused—we all are—his children and yours, too!
But it's your time now—I wish you the best.
Just odd, that's all!
If looks could kill, you say…
Don't judge the look…
Understand the
Situation!

Faces

Be careful how many faces you show…
I'm confused by who you say you are
You appeared to be a gentleman, until life's trials appeared and
your praise turned to curse words. Your smiles turn to snarls

Be careful how many faces you show…
I'm confused by who you say you are
Your moods shift faster than clouds in the sky
You cried in your sleep, and then said you were having bad
dreams. I asked, about your childhood, and you gave me bits and
pieces. Your family described you as having
"A different side."

Be careful how many faces you show…
I'm confused by who you say you are
I didn't know you had a drinking problem. The person on the other
end of the phone had a tongue of pain and hurt, which spread like
venom from a snake's release. You were so accusatory, and so
scared

You said I was like the others
I don't know who the others are because I'm trying to be me. I did
my best to love you, but I couldn't keep up with the personalities
Your faces changed all the time
Many masks

Be careful how many faces you show…
I'm confused by who you say you are.

Section 7
Pain Owns Your Heart

Pain Owns Your Heart

To my son, Jonathan

You have so much hatred toward your
Earthly Father
That you can't hear your
Heavenly Father

You wage a war inside of you
And fail to see
Josiah is the Essence
Of God's Love

Dr. Jekyll & Mr. Hyde

If I wouldn't had given birth to you
I wouldn't know who you are
You say your pain and depression
Introduced you to weed, then that deadly
Devil alcohol sweetly spoke into your ear:
"I got you"

That liquid courage made you an angry
Monster
You had more pain and anger than the
Incredible Hulk
You see, alcohol is a depressant
It makes you cry—laugh—ride an emotional roller coaster

You get suicidal and tell me you're
Here because you promised Mom, Grandma, and Jojo
You asked me why I had you—
It's because you showed me a path to love
You are my gift from God

But you remind me of my dad when he drinks
He has flashbacks of his childhood
All the pain and abuse
Then he headed off to the Vietnam War
He already had PTSD
Now he has
Pain.

Complex Trauma

The cycle of addiction runs deep in our family
I found out later John Hardy—
Your great grandfather—was an alcoholic too

The men in our family drink to numb their pain
And their problems
But the only problem is the pain and problems never go away

The generation of trauma
The holes in your heart and spirit
Only God can heal

Awake
Or take them to your grave
Addictions.

Enablers And Codependent Lovers

Both of my mothers have stood by their husbands
For the past thirty years
My mother stood by her husband up to the time she died of a
Massive heart attack
It was drugs, abuse, and physical and mental pain
That took her life
Or, perhaps she was just tired and relieved—
She died with a smile on her face

I have never understood how a woman can stay
When a man calls out of her name—
You all trigger me
Make me feel unsafe
That's why I can be around you
For only so long
After all this time, you all have gotten older
I have yet to see more love than abuse
Whether it's verbal, mental, or physical
Abuse is Abuse

There are some things I cannot stand
And the main one is abuse
Now that I know better, I choose better
I do better
I saw loving women marry hurt men
Broken men
And yet they stayed by their man's side

I see now that you were teaching them
How to love.

Senseless Violence

Senseless
Makes no sense
Violence
When you no longer see me as a
Human

Deep inside, I have a
Soul, you know
Deep inside, I want the same things you do:
Safety, Protection, Equality
And Justice
Just Us
Trying to be respected
Valued, honored and cherished
A human being
A life, a person, a human
Deep inside I have a soul, too
You know

I'll never understand who gave you the right to take a life
To hunt down black men as animals
Senseless
Violence

Section 8

What Is Happening To The Black Family?

What Is Happening To The Black Family?

Mommy, where's daddy? I have no idea child, go play—Mommy is busy. Busy working, cooking, and caring for the children. Where has it ever been written or said that a woman is supposed to take care of the family alone?

For the men I see hanging in there, I pray God will give you all the anointing to lead, to provide. To care and raise your children in love and pure sacrifice. I pray your wife and children look up to you!

For the men who sought elsewhere—other tribes and religions, please remember you have duties, even if you don't care. Let's stop the use of drugs, disrespecting our God, our races. Let's stop choosing men over women and dismantling the family… and going to prison. Because, brothers, we need you to keep the essence of a strong black family.

The Wisdom Of Our Elders, Titus 2

When did we get so wise that we no longer needed
The council or elders?
What herbs should we use when we are sick? How do we take care
of a woman when she goes through childbirth? How do we
maintain our health? Should we be submissive to our husbands and
wives?

What is the secret of a forty, or fifty, or sixty-year marriage?
How should we prepare our garden? What wisdom do we need to
raise our children? How do we stay out of debt?

The answers come through prayer, my child.
So I stay on my knees!

Passing On The Tradition

Friday night fish fry. BBQ.
Yard work
Exchange vegetables, fresh hen
Eggs
Who slaughtered a cow or pig?

Church

Sunday singing shouting Holy Ghost filled. Dinner after church—
fried chicken, yams, collard greens. Hot water cornbread. Mama,
please—black-eyed peas and okra. Sitting around on the back porch
or the patio porch swing and talking about life. Fanning flies and
smoking rags to kill those bloody mosquitoes. We sat and we
talked. No email, no call waiting. Just a two-way pager. For dessert,
7-Up pound cake. Sock-it-to-me Baby.

No fax machine or mobile. We talked. We sang hymns. We
gathered together in the Lord's Name.
What traditions are you passing along to the next generation?

Pray or Prey

I thought you came to pray with me, then I realized
You came to prey upon
Me

I realized your intentions were evil
The moment you opened your mouth
You spit out venom from every word, phrase, and syllable

You came to prey on my people—
Men, women, and children
Poor, vulnerable, sick, desperate, lonely

I heard they called you Lucifer
Legion evil spirits of many

I thought you came to pray with me
But you came to prey upon me.

Sitting Around The Family Table

Sitting around the family table can prevent divorce. Discuss family issues that are now "none of your business." What goes on in my house, stays in my house. Cancer in the family—don't share the news. Cousin Billie-Joe has AIDS—don't share it. Sista Clara's son is gay—don't share it. Luther is in jail—we don't pray for him because we don't know he was locked up. Mother Lucile is raising five grandchildren—gossip about it, but no one is helping.

Get back around the family table. Come up with a game plan by using the family Bible. Use ten of your best team members to pray. Put the strong men on the front line and put these families back together so we can be there for each other and so our children will know one another.

What Happened At The Family Reunion?

Laughter, hugging, and history.
Please, Uncle Roy, Ray, and Fleming Frazier—don't start no
Domino game. Talking more trash than the law allows. Then Aunt
Cardella cooks catfish, fried okra with hush puppies. Don't forget
the fried green tomatoes! See what you miss when you're not sitting
around the table? Now give me twenty-five on the board and put
some teeny shoes on Him.

Section 9
Healing From The Heart

The Quest

Listen my Brothers and Sister regardless what color you might be
Listen Brothers and Sisters especially those close to me
Think back across troublesome waters to your all-but-forgotten
Roots
Think of all the courage, strength, and pride it took
To fill their thin and weary boots
The seeds of our ancestors were strong, flowing like pieces of pollen
Across the seas unknown
Trying to adapt to a new place and make it
Our home

Generations fell by the way
Shamed, scorned, and buried with feelings of disgrace
But the young seeds continued to grow
Strong, mighty, and without haste
In this new world and in our old homeland—now a dreamland
A distant place

But in this new land we are still fearful—not this America
Our home—and we want our well-earned share
Of this early lot
To plant, cultivate our seed in the same respect
Strength, pride, and unwillingness
Drive to never, never break our
STRIVE
Remember the dream, remember the quest
Strive for your heritage, strive for the best.

Written with Marie Howard (Mama Shirley) July 1989

Healing From The Heart

In 2012, I graduated with my Master's Degree in Social Work
I wanted to start my own counseling services
I was struggling with my own confidence—
Have I done enough personal work
My own counseling
My personal relationship with my Lord?

I had a dream one night
God said, "I need your heart.
That's how you heal."

That's how I got the name of my business—
Healing From The Heart

It's 2016
Thanks for taking a journey with me
The best is yet to come.

The Rocking Chair

I use to bump my head rocking back and forth
They thought something was wrong with me
The doctor said I had a nervous condition
So my mother bought me a rocking chair
No one ever asked what was wrong with me
If they would have asked, I would have told on the ones
Who touched me.

I've had a rocking chair ever since I was a little girl.
The rocking chair was my safe place.
Everyone thought I had a nervous condition, but I start rocking to
Calm myself after
The abuse

When I woke in the morning, everyone thought I was mean and
grumpy, but they couldn't see the dreams that kept me up all night
See, my rocking chair was my safe place. No one touched me and
No one hurt me

Now, I'm 41 and I still have a rocking chair
I still like to rock—it soothes me and calms me down
I pray in my rocking chair
I sing in my rocking chair
My rocking chair is my sanctuary
Now, my son rocks in my rocking chair
He eats in my rocking chair
A lot of people rock in my rocking chair
And when they do, they talk to me and open up about things
I wouldn't dare ask them
You see, my chair is my sanctuary and it soothes and heals me
My chair gives me a peace of mind.

To The Mothers Before Me Who Wrote Poetry, Music To Heal, And Inspired Me

For their healing:
Maya Angelou
Mary J Blige
Oprah Winfrey
Iyanla Vanzant
Jill Scott
Nina Simone
Shirley Caesar
Elizabeth Warren
Rebecca Frazier
All the women of Genesis Fellowship
Mary Mary
Le'Andria Johnson
Yolanda Adams

To The Fathers Before Me—And Current Ones Who Wrote Poetry, Music, Or Spoke To My Life

Eli Whitney
Kirk Franklin
James Baldwin
James Cleveland
Donald Frazier
Fred Hammond

The Books I Read On This Journey

God's Holy Word
Every Woman's Battle, by Shannon Ethridge
Supernatural Transformation, by Guillermo Maldonado
Making Good Habits Breaking Bad Habits, by Joyce Meyer
Battle of the Mind, by Joyce Meyer
No More Sheets, by Juanita Bynum
Saving Our Last Nerve: The African American Women's Path to Mental Health, by Marilyn Martin
I Need your Love—Is that True? by Byron Katie
Loving What Is, by Byron Katie
God Loves Broken People, by Sheila Walsh
Reclaiming Your Real Self: A Psychological and Spiritual Integration, by Rick Johnson Ph.D.
Post Traumatic Slave Syndrome, by Joy DeGruy, Ph.D.
Taming Your Outer Child: Overcoming Self-Sabotage and Healing From Abandonment, by Susan Anderson

The Body Keeps The Score: Brain, Mind, and Body In the Healing of Trauma, by Bessel Van Der Kolk, M.D.

Topics addressed in the writings of Dr. Murray Bowen
Triangles
Differentiation of Self
Nuclear Family Emotional System
Family Projection Process
Multigenerational Transmission Process
Emotional Cutoff
Sibling Position
Societal Emotional Process

About The Author

My name is JAVELIN HARDY. I was born and raised in a small town called Minden, Louisiana. My family moved to Portland, Oregon, during my sophomore year of high school, but I returned to Louisiana to graduate with the friends I'd grown up with. I moved back to Oregon when I was 23 and raised my two sons, who are now 27 and 24 years old. I'm the grandmother of a five-year-old kid I call "King Josiah" because he has an old soul and reminds me of his grandparents.

I began the journey of writing when I was seven years old as I searched for answers about things beyond my imagination. Writing became my sanctuary. I ventured out as I got older and pursued a degree in social work. I took sociology and psychology classes and read a lot of self-care books. I saw counselors who couldn't relate to the things I was trying to express—trapped as a women by what the little girl inside me had seen and suffered from. It wasn't until I started studying how drugs and alcohol cause turmoil in families that I understood why I had not been protected and why I did not feel safe as a child. I also studied my family history of various addictions and dysfunctions.

Through my relationship with God, a healing transformation began. I gave God every memory of my pain. I prayed, *Please take this journey with me and get ready, for there is more to come.* We all have secrets. We're set free only when we reveal them. Writing them down, or speaking the words out loud, gives us peace of mind.

JAVELIN HARDY, CSWA, is a Master Level Social Worker, Qualified Mental Health Professional, and Clinical Social Worker Associate. She received her Master's Degree in Social Work from Portland State University in 2012. She's has twenty-three year's experience working with adults with mental health and substance abuse issues, and with their families. She has extensive experience working with the adult justice systems, courts, and the State Health and Human Service system.

Her private practice, Healing from the Heart, is a multicultural, adult counseling service that provides individual therapy, group therapy, family therapy, and couples therapy.

Her family served in the US Military for five generations, and Javelin herself served in the Oregon National Guard. As a result, she is familiar with military culture and lifestyles, and provides counseling services to military veterans and their families.

Her areas of specialty include anxiety, depression, women's emotional health, trauma related to PTSD, and healing from substance abuse and dependence. She is certified in various trauma-informed methods. She ties Yoga and various relaxation methods into her treatment practice. She believes in a holistic approach to health.

A special thank you to
Cornell Gray

my best friend
who understood me in high school